# Intermezzo, op. 118 no. 2

J. Brahms
arr. William Ransom
for Laura

2

4

# JOHANNES BRAHMS

## INTERMEZZO FOR CLARINET & PIANO
## Op. 118 No. 2

*Arranged by William Ransom*
*Edited by Richard Stoltzman*

### CLARINET

**Concert A version**
Clarinet in A .................... 2
Clarinet in Bb .................. 4

**Concert Bb version**
Clarinet in Bb .................. 6

Performance notes ........ 8

LAUREN KEISER
MUSIC PUBLISHING

Clarinet in A

# Intermezzo, op. 118 no. 2

J. Brahms
arr. William Ransom
for Laura

Clarinet in A

Clarinet in B♭

# Intermezzo, op. 118 no. 2

J. Brahms
arr. William Ransom
for Laura

Clarinet in B♭

Clarinet in B♭

# Intermezzo, op. 118 no. 2

J. Brahms
arr. William Ransom
for Laura

Clarinet in B♭

*Performance notes by Richard Stoltzman*

In the span of three years, Brahms composed a veritable treasure trove of clarinet music. First came the *Trio*, Op. 114, which was followed in the same year by the *Quintet*, Op. 115 (1891). Then, in 1894 he gave us his Sonatas: Op. 120 No. 1 &2. Nestled amidst these fervid works is the melancholy *Intermezzo*, Op. 118 No. 2 (1893). Though written for the piano, one can easily imagine the memory of Richard Mühfeld, Brahms' "nightengale" of the clarinet, haunting the melodic lines which seem to flow so effortlessly. Just sing the melody of the first four measures in your mind and you will hold them forever. Brahms asks for an *andante teneramente*, a desire to linger tenderly within the graceful intervals. What better instrument to do this than clarinet, with its infinite dynamics, its breathing sonorities? Think of the final return of the graceful ländler in the 3rd movement of the first clarinet Sonata, Op. 120, No.1. That special request *"teneramente,"* appears just after the pause ending the trio. That sense of reflection on what has gone before permeates this lovely transcription by William Ransom, Professor of piano at Emory University.

Before you play your clarinet part, look through the score, trace the shapes of lines, find the shifts in key centers from major to relative minor (at the first double bar), to major on that same tone (after the repeat) at *piu lento*. Brahms makes full use of *crescendo* and *diminuendo* signs, he asks us for a *dolce* quality six times, *espressivo* three times, and many fluctuations in tempi, and dynamic extremes from *pianissimo* to *forte*. Obviously Brahms is asking us to search for meaning in every measure and magically, almost mystically, ends this short yet soulful work with the same melody as the beginning, now in the subdued chalumeau.

# Intermezzo, op. 118 no. 2

Full Score

J. Brahms
arr. William Ransom
for Laura

*Performance notes by Richard Stoltzman*

In the span of three years, Brahms composed a veritable treasure trove of clarinet music. First came the *Trio*, Op. 114, which was followed in the same year by the *Quintet*, Op. 115 (1891). Then, in 1894 he gave us his Sonatas: Op. 120 No. 1 &2. Nestled amidst these fervid works is the melancholy *Intermezzo*, Op. 118 No. 2 (1893). Though written for the piano, one can easily imagine the memory of Richard Mühfeld, Brahms' "nightengale" of the clarinet, haunting the melodic lines which seem to flow so effortlessly. Just sing the melody of the first four measures in your mind and you will hold them forever. Brahms asks for an *andante teneramente*, a desire to linger tenderly within the graceful intervals. What better instrument to do this than clarinet, with its infinite dynamics, its breathing sonorities? Think of the final return of the graceful ländler in the 3rd movement of the first clarinet Sonata, Op. 120, No.1. That special request "*teneramente*," appears just after the pause ending the trio. That sense of reflection on what has gone before permeates this lovely transcription by William Ransom, Professor of piano at Emory University.

Before you play your clarinet part, look through the score, trace the shapes of lines, find the shifts in key centers from major to relative minor (at the first double bar), to major on that same tone (after the repeat) at *piu lento*. Brahms makes full use of *crescendo* and *diminuendo* signs, he asks us for a *dolce* quality six times, *espressivo* three times, and many fluctuations in tempi, and dynamic extremes from *pianissimo* to *forte*. Obviously Brahms is asking us to search for meaning in every measure and magically, almost mystically, ends this short yet soulful work with the same melody as the beginning, now in the subdued chalumeau.